RYAN'S WORLD OF SCIENCE

Ready-to-Read

Simon Spotlight
New York   London   Toronto   Sydney   New Delhi

While the following experiments don't pose any significant safety hazards, all activities should have proper safety precautions and adult supervision.

SIMON SPOTLIGHT
An imprint of Simon & Schuster Children's Publishing Division
1230 Avenue of the Americas, New York, New York 10020
This Simon Spotlight edition January 2021
Text by Aubre Andrus
For information about special discounts for bulk purchases, please contact Simon & Schuster Special Sales at 1-866-506-1949 or business@simonandschuster.com.
Manufactured in the United States of America 1020 LAK
2 4 6 8 10 9 7 5 3 1
ISBN 978-1-5344-6811-5 (hc)
ISBN 978-1-5344-6810-8 (pbk)
ISBN 978-1-5344-6812-2 (eBook)

Hi! I am Ryan,
and I love science.

HELLO!

Do you want to do science
experiments with me?
Let's go!

EXPERIMENT:
WHY DO APPLE SLICES TURN BROWN?

I put five apple slices
in different places.

Some slices turned brown.
Some slices did not.
Why?

TRY THE EXPERIMENT YOURSELF!

YOU WILL NEED:

- 1 apple
- 4 see-through containers, like cups or bowls
- aluminum foil

Always do the experiment with a grown-up.

1. Ask a grown-up to cut the apple into five slices.
2. Put four slices into four containers.
3. Place the containers in these places:

on a table or counter

in the fridge

in a dark place

outside

4. Tightly wrap the fifth apple slice with aluminum foil. Place it on a table or counter.

5. Which apple slices will turn brown? Make a guess!

6. Wait for one day. Then look at all the apple slices. Which ones turned brown? Was your guess correct?

COUNTER

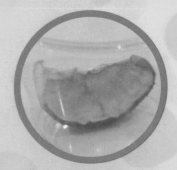

OUTSIDE

IN THE DARK

IN THE FRIDGE

ALUMINUM FOIL

Do you know why some slices turned brown and some of them did not?

Apples turn brown when they touch the air. Bananas and avocados turn brown too. This is called oxidation (say: OCK-suh-DAY-shun).

There are some ways
to slow down oxidation.
Cold places like the fridge can
slow it down.
A tight lid or wrapper that keeps
air out can also slow it down.

That is why the covered apple slice and the slice in the fridge did not turn brown.
Yum!

EXPERIMENT:
HOW DOES WATER WALK?

Want to see something cool?
I can make water walk
from one place to another.

I can also make a rainbow
at the same time!

COOL!

TRY THE EXPERIMENT YOURSELF!

YOU WILL NEED:

- 7 see-through cups
- red, yellow, blue, and purple food coloring
- 6 paper towels
- water
- a stirring utensil, like a spoon or a popsicle stick

Always do the experiment with a grown-up.

1. Fill four cups with water.
2. Add one drop of red food coloring to the first cup. Then add one drop of yellow food coloring to the second cup, one drop of blue to the third cup, and one drop of purple to the fourth cup.
3. Stir the water in each cup.

4. Place an empty cup between each cup filled with colored water.

5. Take six paper towels. Fold each one lengthwise in half. Then fold it in half again.

6. Put one end of the paper towel in a colored water cup and the other end in an empty cup next to it. Repeat until each cup is connected to the cups next to it.

7. What do you think will happen?
   Make a guess! Then wait a few hours.

Can you see the water
walking up the paper towel?
Wait a little longer.
Now it is walking down
into the empty cup!

By the next day,
the empty cups
will have water inside.
And you will have a rainbow of
colored water.

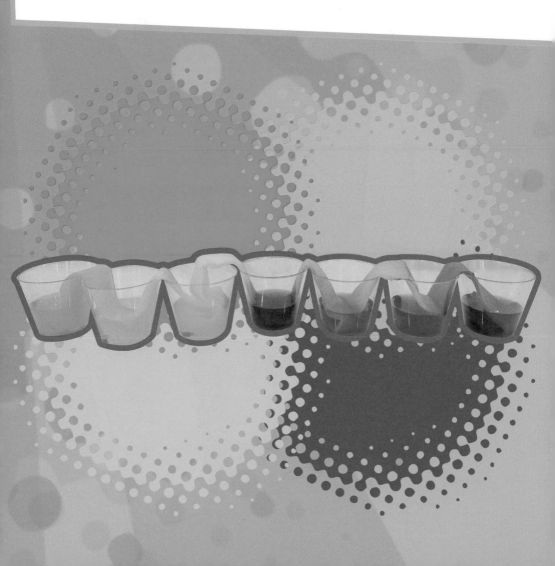

This experiment shows capillary action
(say: KAP-uh-leh-ree AK-shun).

Capillary action helps water travel up thin places like straws, plants, and paper towels.
It is not magic.
It is science!

EXPERIMENT:
HOW DO OBJECTS SINK OR FLOAT?

Here is a coin.

It sinks!

Here is a cap.

It floats!

Want to find out why?

TRY THE EXPERIMENT YOURSELF!

YOU WILL NEED:

- water
- any kind of syrup, like corn or maple syrup
- any kind of cooking oil
- 1 large see-through container, like a jar or fishbowl
- 3 small objects, like a coin, a Ping-Pong ball, and a cherry tomato. Pick objects that you do not mind getting dirty!
- food coloring (if you want it)

Always do the experiment with a grown-up.

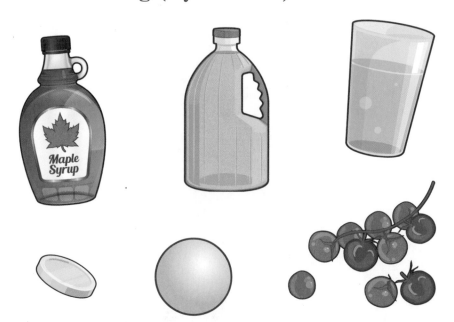

1. Pour water into the container until it is about one-quarter filled. You can add a drop of green food coloring so that it is easier to see the water.
2. Pour the same amount of syrup into the container.
3. Pour the same amount of cooking oil into the container.
4. Wait for ten minutes. What happened?

OIL

WATER

SYRUP

5. Guess if each object will sink or float inside the container.
6. Drop each object, one at a time, into the container. Were your guesses correct?

What makes objects
sink or float?
Density (say: DEN-sih-tee)!
Density depends on the size
and weight of an object.

Objects that are more dense sink. Objects that are less dense float.

LEAST DENSE

MORE DENSE THAN
OIL, LESS DENSE
THAN SYRUP

MOST DENSE

A coin is more dense than
water, oil, and syrup,
so it sinks.

A Ping-Pong ball is less
dense than water, oil,
and syrup, so it floats.

A tomato is more dense than water and oil.
But it is less dense than syrup, so it does not sink all the way.
Wow!

PING-PONG BALL

TOMATO

COIN

Science is so much fun.
I love learning new things
every day!

See you again soon!

DEAR PARENTS AND CAREGIVERS,

I'm Loann, Ryan's mom. When I was a science teacher, there was one thing I always wanted my students to know: that science is everywhere! Whether your child is playing at a park or swimming in a pool, they are interacting with science.

Science is in your home, too! These experiments in this book are stress-free and easy to do at home—you probably already own all the materials. I love doing science experiments with Ryan at home on the weekends. It's a fun way to spend time together while Ryan learns new concepts and grows his observational skills.

Wherever you are, nurture your budding scientist by encouraging them to ask a lot of questions. It's okay if you don't know the answers. What's important is that your child is curious about the world around them. Who

knows? Maybe you'll learn something new along the way too!

I hope you and your child have fun doing these experiments. Ryan and I had a blast. Science rocks!

-LOANN